POSTCARD HISTORY SERIES

Florida Railroads

Seth H. Bramson

ARCADIA
PUBLISHING

Copyright © 2019 by Seth H. Bramson
ISBN 978-1-4671-0364-0

Published by Arcadia Publishing
Charleston, South Carolina

Library of Congress Control Number: 2019931063

For all general information contact Arcadia Publishing at:
Telephone 843-853-2070
Fax 843-853-0044
E-mail sales@arcadiapublishing.com
For customer service and orders:
Toll-Free 1-888-313-2665

Visit us on the Internet at www.arcadiapublishing.com

CONTENTS

ACKNOWLEDGMENTS

All postcards in this book are from the Bramson Archive.

INTRODUCTION

While it has often been said that "Florida could not have become Florida without its railroads," that statement can easily apply to most of the country. But Florida, as with so many other things, in terms of the history of its railroads, is completely unique.

The stories of the three Henrys (Flagler, Plant, and Sanford) and what they did to build the state and its tourism are part of Florida's lore and legend and, for the most part, are completely true. Although Sanford's role is not as extraordinary as Flagler's and Plant's, his contributions, particularly in Central Florida, are major. Plant, of course, was the Henry Flagler of the west coast and Central Florida, but unquestionably, the single greatest name in the history of the state is that of Flagler's.

Railroad building in the Panhandle cannot be overlooked either, and this book certainly includes that section of the state as well as all the rest, but I must ask readers to be aware that even with 211 photographs in this book, it was simply not possible to include all or even most of the railroad postcard views that exist, which number in the thousands. I have attempted to include every part of the state, from Fernandina Beach to Jacksonville and west to Pensacola as well as from Jacksonville south and southwest so that locales throughout the state are among the numerous postcards shown.

Yes, it was difficult to choose which postcards from which roads would be used. My collection includes two full file boxes of FEC postcards, one full box of other Florida railroad postcards, and one full box of street and electric railway postcards; hence, the concern was not whether or not the postcards were available, but rather, which ones would be shown. It is therefore important that those perusing this book recognize that it was simply impossible to "show them all," for "all" would encompass thousands of different views. I have, therefore, chosen those that I thought (and hoped) would be of the greatest interest to the largest number of Florida railfans, buffs, and historians, because this book is for anybody and everybody who has an interest not just in the state's railroads but also in the history of the Sunshine State.

As with so many other places and so many other topics, the story of the railroads of the Sunshine State can be and is often told by including postcards. Historians and researchers have in many cases found that a given site, scene, or building has been preserved only through one or more postcard images; in this book, readers will see a number of views that have never before been published. *Florida Railroads* presents an entirely new and different perspective of the history of the railroads of Florida.

Without the railroads, Florida would certainly exist, but would it have become the third-most populous state in the country? Highly doubtful, and I hope and trust that everyone who reads this book will gain a greater feeling not only for the state's colorful and dynamic history but also for the part that its railroads have played in making it all possible. Now, dear readers, sit back, enjoy, and be enveloped by the past and the present of the Sunshine State.

Arrived at Jacksonville, Fla.

Jacksonville was either the meeting point or the terminal station for trains of the Atlantic Coast Line (ACL), FEC, and Seaboard Air Line (SAL), as well as several Louisville & Nashville–SAL joint trains, a number of Southern Railway and subsidiary, the Georgia Southern & Florida services, one train with through sleeping cars, and one or more coaches that originated in Kansas City on the St. Louis–San Francisco Railway and terminated in Jacksonville with the through cars continuing to Miami on the FEC during the winter season. Because of the angle of the train shown on this postcard, it cannot be determined if this was an ACL, SAL, or Southern Railway consist, but what is certain is that this great image was made at the old Jacksonville Terminal, which would be replaced by the new facility in 1919.

One

ATLANTIC COAST LINE RAILROAD

As in many other states, the largest railroads generally emerged from a series of buyouts, mergers, or through-operations partnerships, and so it was in Florida. The Atlantic Coast Line and the Seaboard Air Line Railroads were perfect examples of all three types of consolidations, the ACL, for the most part, having taken over through purchase in 1902 the numerous smaller lines of the Plant System. The ACL bought the several roads that had been part of that system from Henry Plant's widow and son that year.

Atlantic Coast Line service to, from, and within Florida began through its predecessor, the Plant System, as early as 1888 with the origination of the all–first class sleeping car train, the New York & Florida Special, later to become the Florida Special, for many years known as "the Aristocrat of Winter Trains." Initially operating from Exchange Place Terminal in Jersey City, the train was extended to New York City when Pennsylvania Station opened in 1909. That train, incidentally, would eventually have through sleeping cars to Key West on the FEC.

The ACL spread throughout Florida, its lines providing service from the southernmost reaches of the state, including Naples (after that line was purchased from the SAL), Everglades City, and Clewiston on the south side of Lake Okeechobee. East coast service, until the FEC strike began on January 22, 1963, was provided for all of the Coast Line's through trains to Miami via the FEC.

ACL depots were of a wide variety of architectural styles, and some of them are shown in this chapter as well as in chapter seven.

As will be noted in the captions of the postcards of the FEC and SAL predecessors, those cards are very difficult to come by, primarily because only real-photo postcards, which are images taken by a photographer and then made into postcards, exist. The first example of a predecessor postcard is this engineer's side view of Plant System 4-6-0 No. 117, built for the Savannah, Florida & Western, one of the Plant System's many operating entities. This engine later became ACL No. 1295.

Here, passenger train No. 82 was involved in an accident at Davenport. This view shows the first four cars of the train looking forward toward the locomotive. The two passenger cars appear to be of wooden construction. The postcard states that the wreck occurred on April 6 but does not include the year.

A different view of the same accident, taken from the other side and looking rearward, shows a steel railway post office (RPO) car, which is preceded by a steel baggage car; hence, it is likely that the accident occurred sometime in the mid-1920s.

A.C.L. TRAIN ON WEST MAIN STREET, GAINESVILLE, FLA.

In a number of US cities, passenger and freight trains operated right down the middle of a busy and often crowded thoroughfare. West Main Street in Gainesville was one such right-of-way; the six-car passenger train shown here is cautiously making its way toward that city's passenger station.

View of A. C. L. Ry. Wharf from a point in front of Warehouse, showing a few Fish Packing houses to the left, Punta Gorda, Fla. Hotel Punta Gorda appears in the distance.

The Coast Line owned and operated "public" piers or wharfs, complete with freight and or passenger train service on them, in several cities. This fascinating view of the ACL wharf in Punta Gorda shows not only fish packinghouses on the left but also the Punta Gorda Hotel, one of the hostelries of the Plant System before it was sold, in the distance on the right.

Fishing on A. C. L. Dock, St. Petersburg, Fla.

In St. Petersburg, fishing was allowed by the railroad on its dock. With fishermen (and women) in abundance in the foreground on the dock, the masts of several sailing vessels are prominent on the opposite side.

Atlantic Coast Line, St. Petersburg, Fla., Station and Famous PINELLAS SPECIAL operated between Jacksonville and St. Petersburg.

The Pinellas Special was one of three trains that operated daily between St. Petersburg and Jacksonville. Engine No. 397, leading an eight-car train, is adorned with antlers on its headlight, a personalization then allowed by the railroad to those enginemen who operated the same locomotive on a regular basis.

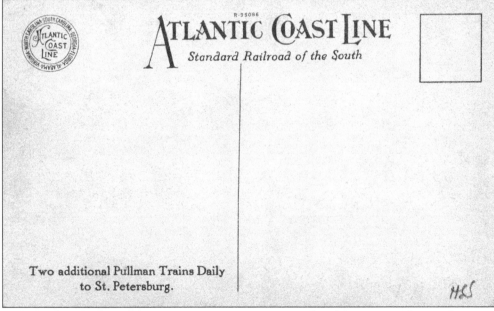

In the heyday of rail passenger train operations, competing railroads in major markets, such as New York or Chicago to Miami, often provided passengers with complimentary advertising material. The back of the previous postcard, complete with the ACL name and emblem, as well as the notation that there were two additional Pullman sleeping car trains daily to St. Petersburg, notes that the ACL was the "Standard Railroad of the South," which was a play on the Pennsylvania Railroad referring to itself as "the Standard Railroad of the World."

Passenger Depot, LAKELAND, FLA.

Lakeland was a major division point for both freight and passenger trains. Over the years, the city had three different passenger stations, the first one shown in this c. 1905 postcard view. This card shows not only the engine, which is taking on water, but also the large Western Union Telegraph Company sign at the end of the building.

Atlantic Coast Line Railroad Passenger and Freight Terminal, Lakeland, Florida

The third Lakeland depot, built in Mid-Century Modern architectural style, is shown here. Not only did most trains from the west coast stop here en route to Jacksonville, but this station was also the terminal for the trains heading south to Naples, those lasting until the start of Amtrak in 1971.

A. C. L. Depot, Winter Park, Fla.

Winter Park is still in use as a regular stop for Amtrak trains. The original depot was a busy place, with several trains a day stopping there.

O.129—A. C. L. Railway Station, Orlando, Fla.
"The City Beautiful"

Even pre–Walt Disney World, Orlando was worthy of a major depot. Shown in ACL's beautiful purple paint scheme, a long passenger train is braking to a stop preparatory to loading a large number of passengers.

MUSIC DANCING HOSTESS GAMES

For the 1935–1936 winter season, the Florida Special became the only passenger train in American history to ever carry a swimming pool. This postcard, available to passengers in either the mid-train lounge car or the observation car at the rear of the train, portrayed the various entertainments available on that train between New York and Miami.

Here, a two-unit ACL diesel set in the company's 500 series of passenger locomotives is waiting to depart St. Petersburg. That city's station is the two-story building directly behind the train. Note the plane included in the postcard.

A three-unit set of passenger diesels awaits the call at Jacksonville Terminal in 1957. It appears, given the location of the units, that the engineer, looking rearward from the cab, is awaiting the highball to head north.

Port Tampa was built by Henry Plant to make Tampa the great Florida west coast port. The Gulf Oil Refinery Works were a mainstay of freight traffic to and from the port, first for the Plant System and then for the Coast Line.

The caption on the front of this postcard is "Speedy New York–Florida Streamliner," and the Champion truly was. Inaugurated with 25.5-hour service between New York City and Miami, the all-coach train carried a dining car and a tavern-lounge observation car and was the ACL's answer to the Seaboard's Silver Meteor, which started service a year earlier, in 1938.

For its 75th anniversary in 1962–1963, the Florida Special, even though having had coaches added, brought new luxury to the rails with champagne dinners, movies, and onboard fashion shows. With the start of the strike by FEC nonoperating employees on January 22, 1963, the train operated into Miami on the Seaboard and the great days of FEC passenger train service effectively came to an end.

Two

FLORIDA EAST COAST RAILWAY

It is possible, if not likely, that more words have been written about and more books published on the Florida East Coast Railway (FEC) and its history than any other regional railroad in America. Five books, including three published by Arcadia and The History Press, have been written by this author, and the FEC is the only railroad in the country with an officially titled company historian, which should be no surprise to any fan or aficionado of that incredible railroad.

With its original predecessor having been purchased by Henry M. Flagler on December 31, 1885, the FEC and its associated companies have been almost completely responsible for the development of much, if not most, of Florida's east coast. The attributions include the founding of numerous cities, including Miami, West Palm Beach, Hallandale, Dania, and many more; the building, buying, or leasing of hotels along the east coast, including two in the Bahamas; the ownership of several land companies, which enabled thousands of people to purchase property on the east coast at reasonable prices; and the employing, during and throughout the FEC's history, of many thousands of men and women who helped to build and promote the east coast's infrastructure.

The FEC has survived booms, busts, a 30-year bankruptcy, a 13-year strike by nonoperating employees, sabotage, vicious hurricanes, changes in ownership, and the rebuilding of itself from the ground up. Now owned by Grupo México, the company is headed by Nathan "Nate" Asplund, a man whose focus on increasing both the level of business and the company's imprint and recognition in its home state goes hand in hand with preserving the railroad's extraordinary history. With his experience in and knowledge of the railroad business, Nate Asplund, a great historian in his own right, is the perfect person for the job at hand.

The FEC is "Florida's railroad," and no American railway has ever been more closely identified or associated with a single state than the FEC. So it has always been, so it shall always continue to be.

Most of the predecessor railroads of the state's "big three," the ACL, FEC, and Seaboard, had been subsumed, merged into, or taken over, at least for the most part, prior to the advent of commercial postcard production, hence a postcard of a predecessor road is rare. Fortunately, at some point, an unidentified photographer shot the engineer's side of Jacksonville, St. Augustine & Halifax River Railroad 4-4-0 No. 10, and the negative was used to make this very rare real-photo postcard of that locomotive, one of the few postcard images of any of the Florida railroads' predecessors known to exist.

4-6-0 No. 40 was built in 1902 and was sold and off the property by 1925. Apparently being used as a switch engine at the railroad's St. Augustine station, shops, and yard, No. 40, in this undated real-photo postcard, is shown on the trackage on the west side of the St. Augustine depot with five unidentified employees standing next to it.

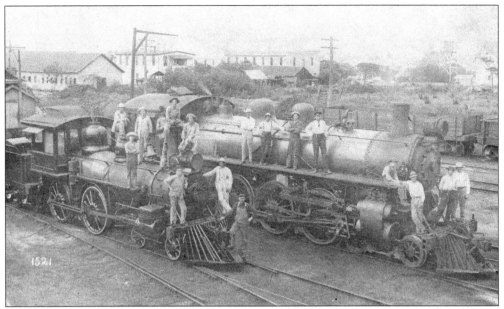

The reason for this posed real-photo postcard, taken by Fort Pierce's Florida Photographic Concern in that city's FEC yard, is unknown. However, the 4-4-0 at left is No. 10 and was used as a Key West switch engine during the construction of the extension. The 4-6-2's numbers on the headlight and the front number plate are just too indistinct to read. However, FEC employee Howard "Kid" Matthews, whose name is on the back of the card, is likely one of those shown.

Railroad Bridge across Lake Worth,
West Palm Beach, Fla.

After the railroad reached West Palm Beach, the decision was made to cross Lake Worth on the south side of the FEC Hotel Company's Royal Poinciana Hotel in order to reach Palm Beach and serve both of the company's hotels on the island. After Flagler married his third wife, the former Mary Lily Kenan, she complained that the trains were disturbing her sleep, so he closed that trestle and built this one to the north of the hotel. The trackage on the island was, however, kept in place in order to initiate an animal-powered trolley service between the two hotels.

Palm Beach Rapid Transit, Palm Beach, Fla.

The mule car that operated every winter season between the Royal Poinciana and the Breakers Hotel was, according to the Palm Beach Historical Society, kept in service until 1928. When the service was discontinued, the Palm Beach trolley was the very last railroad-owned, animal-powered trolley or streetcar in America.

Knights Key Dock, showing the new steel bridge which will connect Knights Key with Pidgeon Key.
Compliments of the Land Department of the Florida East Coast Railway, St. Augustine, Florida.

As noted in the caption of the first photograph in this book, the FEC's Key West Extension was a feat like no other. Because the completion of the railroad to Key West was held up for three years due to issues relating to the filling for the Key West terminal, a temporary dock was built off Knights Key, three-eighths of a mile into the Atlantic Ocean. A "Compliments of the Land Department of the Florida East Coast Railway" series postcard showing the trestle used to reach Knights Key is the subject of this card.

The marvelous Ocean Railway. To the Island City, Key West, Fla. Showing method of Construction.

Much of the construction required new and innovative techniques, including the building of bridges and viaducts requiring a series of arches, as part of the engineering process. One of those bridges, likely Long Key Viaduct, is shown in this very rare postcard from "the marvelous Ocean Railway" series published by the Rotograph Company of New York City and printed in Germany.

F.E.C. VIADUCT
PIGEON KEY, FLA.

At Pigeon Key, the railroad soared over the island on trestlework. That location served for some years as a supply depot and dormitory for the workers. The FEC's buildings are shown on either side of the viaduct.

The author is in possession of a series of real-photo postcards made by the great author Zane Grey, who brought the Long Key Fishing Camp (LKFC) to national prominence, serving as president of the Long Key Fishing Club in the late 1920s and early 1930s. He took this photograph of his family and lady friends on the ocean side of the fishing camp's lodge.

Because the train on the Long Key Viaduct shown on this postcard is only four cars long and the locomotive is of the American Standard 4-4-0 type, it appears that the photograph was taken and the card made within a year or so of the Key West Extension's opening.

During the extension's construction, the railroad commissioned a series of postcards titled "F.E.C. Ry. Extension Series." Published by the Rose Co., this card, No. 42 in the series, shows the scale of the Long Key Viaduct with a number of workers standing atop.

Florida East Coast Railway, Key West Extension. Train crossing Bahia Honda Bridge, Florida.

Because the water below the Bahia Honda Bridge was as much as 45 feet deep, that crossing was the only one on the extension with steel girders on either side, preventing a locomotive or cars from going "into the drink" in the unlikely occurrence of a collision or derailment on the bridge. Fortunately, during the 23-plus years of the extension, no such accident occurred there.

The terminal at Trumbo Point, Key West, was 522 miles from Jacksonville, and it was at Trumbo that FEC passenger trains made close connections in either direction with the steamships to and from Havana. The engine shown is either No. 121, No. 122, or No. 123, all 4-6-2 Pacific-type locomotives used regularly on the passenger trains to and from the island city. The SS *Mascotte*, of the Flagler System's and ACL's jointly owned P&O Steamship Company, is dockside.

Souvenir Folder of
SCENES ÁLONG THE
OVERSEA RÁILROAD,
KEY WEST EXTENSION
FLORIDA.

From E. F. L. /

Mr. John F. Littlefield
Ward 32
Essex Co. Hospital
Cedar Grove
N. J.

There were few rail trips in American history as exciting as the ride on the Oversea Railway. The name was never "Overseas"—the railroad did not go "overseas," but it did go over the sea to Key West. Innumerable travelers sent postcards or postcard folders, such as the one shown here, to the folks at home. This folder was cancelled at Long Key (the post office was one of the buildings at the LKFC) and carried on one of the FEC's trains on August 29, 1932. Note the George Washington one and a half cent stamp!

FEC DEPOT 1957
SOUTH BAY, FLA.

Because several of the branch lines went to and through rural areas that were akin to wilderness, with living quarters many miles from the assigned depots, a number of the stations were two stories, as shown here. The agent and his family lived upstairs. By the look of the car and the air-conditioner in the second-story window, it is safe to assume that this real-photo postcard of South Bay station on the Kissimmee Valley branch was made sometime in the mid-1950s.

Considered one of the nation's finest railroad photographers and one of the greatest in Florida history, company photographer Harry M. Wolfe photographed the FEC as a full-time employee from 1925 until his retirement in 1958. This photograph, made with his Graflex camera at Miami station during the 1935–1936 season and used for publicity purposes as a postcard, shows three of the four sections of train No. 88, the all-Pullman sleeping car Florida Special, each with a band playing on the back platform and its own hostess, preparing to leave the summer climes of South Florida for the wintry blasts of Manhattan and points between.

53:—FLORIDA SPECIAL,
MIAMI, FLA.

DADE COUNTY COURT HOUSE
IN BACKGROUND.

In April 1935, one of the FEC's "greyhounds," the powerful, high-speed Mountain-type 4-8-2 No. 442 is ready to depart New Smyrna Beach with a long train of heavyweight, all-steel cars en route south to Miami, or possibly Key West. The station is the two-story building behind the third and fourth cars.

In December 1939, the FEC received its first streamlined, diesel-powered train, the Henry M. Flagler, named, of course, for the road's founder. The train's daily Jacksonville–Miami round-trip schedule was so tight that it was serviced at the Miami station, rather than being taken to Buena Vista Yard as all the other trains were. One hour and one minute were allowed for servicing in Miami, which included cleaning the train, restocking the diner and lounge cars, and refueling the engine.

Florida East Coast Railway Streamliner 263
Enroute Through The Land Of Palms

This FEC publicity postcard featuring the Henry M. Flagler shows the train at an unidentified station. Although thousands came out to view the train at its inauguration, ridership was paltry, and in 1941, the train, in concert with three of the FEC's connections (ACL, L&N, and Chicago & Eastern Illinois), became the Dixie Flagler, a through Chicago–Miami all-coach streamliner.

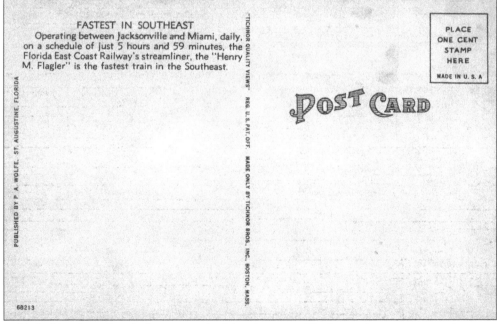

FASTEST IN SOUTHEAST

Operating between Jacksonville and Miami, daily, on a schedule of just 5 hours and 59 minutes, the Florida East Coast Railway's streamliner, the "Henry M. Flagler" is the fastest train in the Southeast.

PUBLISHED BY P. A. WOLFE, ST. AUGUSTINE, FLORIDA

"TICHNOR QUALITY VIEWS" REG. U.S. PAT. OFF. MADE ONLY BY TICHNOR BROS. INC., BOSTON, MASS.

POST CARD

PLACE
ONE CENT
STAMP
HERE

MADE IN U. S. A

68213

Published by the railroad, this postcard of the Henry M. Flagler passing a coconut palm states that the train was the fastest in the Southeast. Incredibly, it operated from Jacksonville to Miami (and reverse—365 miles in each direction) on a daily schedule, except on Sunday, in five hours and 59 minutes, with one hour and one minute allowed for servicing in Miami. Incredibly, the train made 18 intermediate stops between the terminals.

Florida East Coast Railway

Built in the mid-1920s to replace the former general office building, which then became the passenger annex, these three four-story buildings have been a St. Augustine landmark since then. When the railroad moved its offices to Jacksonville in the 1980s, an arrangement was made with Flagler College to take over the property, and the school now owns and operates the buildings as dormitories and classrooms. The transparency used to make this postcard was made by Werner Bertsch.

Three

SEABOARD AIR LINE AND SEABOARD COAST LINE RAILROADS

The Seaboard, as did the ACL and the FEC, did the same thing as far as its growth through the years. Until the extensions to Naples on the west coast and Miami and Homestead on the east coast added several hundred miles to the railroad in 1925, the largest part of that system in Florida was made up of the routes of the former Florida Central & Peninsula Railroad (FC&P), which the Seaboard purchased in 1900.

The Seaboard, as did the Coast Line, had major port facilities in Jacksonville, Tampa, and Fernandina, which was the east coast terminal of the original Florida Railroad, the first cross-state line that had been built by David Levy Yulee, Florida's first US senator after the territory became a state in 1845. On July 1, 1967, the Seaboard merged with the Atlantic Coast Line to become the Seaboard Coast Line Railroad. Both roads are now, as a result of the merger with the Baltimore & Ohio–Chesapeake & Ohio network, a part of CSX Transportation.

Known for both fast freight and fast passenger trains, the Seaboard, upon the opening of its lines to Naples and Miami, initiated the famed Orange Blossom Special, a winter-only all-Pullman sleeping car luxury train, which competed directly with the ACL–FEC Florida Special. The SAL inaugurated the first New York–Florida diesel-electric streamlined train, the Silver Meteor, in December 1938. Several years later, that train was joined by the Silver Star, serving the same cities as the Silver Meteor but on a slightly slower schedule. All three of those trains served both Florida coasts, as did the ACL trains. In 1954, SAL president John W. Smith decided not to streamline the Orange Blossom Special, and that train was then discontinued.

The Seaboard, for several years, ran a cross-Florida day train, as well as a night train on the same route, from Miami to Tampa. Another SAL route took freight and passengers from Jacksonville to River Junction, connecting there with the Louisville & Nashville Railroad in a through-service arrangement, which took passengers (and freight destined for that city and points west) through to New Orleans. Although now a part of CSX Transportation, the Seaboard is memorialized through the membership and activities of the ACL & SAL Railroads Historical Society, which, like the FEC Railway Society, holds a yearly convention and puts out a fine and high-grade magazine on a regular basis.

The Seaboard's largest predecessor in Florida was the FC&P, and as with the ACL's or FEC's Florida predecessors, postcards are rare but will surface on occasion. This real-photo postcard, taken at an unknown location, depicts four employees with FC&P 4-4-0 No. 13.

This marvelously rare real-photo postcard provides a look at a c. 1898–1904 Zephyrhills. "There are no zephyrs and there are no hills in Zephyrhills," according to the spring water producer of the same name. Visible in the foreground are two Seaboard wooden boxcars with No. 23627 at right. The building in the background on the right might have been a hotel.

FOUR YEAR OLD GRAPEFRUIT TREE IN THE LAND OF MANATEE. FLORIDA
ALONG SEABOARD AIR LINE RAILWAY

Following the Naples and Miami/Homestead extensions, the Seaboard strongly promoted its new lines and the surrounding territory. While the front of this card shows a "Four Year Old Grapefruit Tree in the Land of Manatee, Florida" (likely Manatee County on the west coast), the back is preprinted. Addressed to the railroad's general industrial agent in Norfolk, Virginia, it requests, "Facts concerning farms and homes . . . along the Seaboard Air Line Railway."

Seminole Indian Village—Miami, Fla.

This green-tinted postcard was later a promotional piece, complimentary on those trains with lounge cars and in the railroad's ticket offices. Complete with a promotional blurb on the back, the picture on the front is of seven Seminole Indian children posing for the photographer at a "Seminole Indian Village–Miami, Fla."

Loading Phosphate at Seaboard Dock, Tampa, Fla.

Surprisingly, Florida had a large number of phosphate mines in the area east of Tampa, including Polk County. The Seaboard dock in Tampa was a major transshipping point and was always busy with freighters being loaded with that mineral.

FIRST PASSENGER TRAIN TO BURBANK, FLA.

Burbank, Florida, is near Fort McCoy, an unincorporated community in Marion County, northeast of Ocala between the towns of Sparr and Eureka on County Road 316 directly north of Silver Springs on County Road 315. Every town in the late 1800s and early 1900s believed that a railroad would bring growth, fame, and fortune, and so it was with Burbank, shown here with its first Seaboard train.

Scene showing S.A.L. Railway Station and Arrival of New York Special Tourists Train at Boca Grande, Florida

The Charlotte Harbor & Northern (CH&N) Railroad was another SAL predecessor in Florida. A long CH&N extension brought freight and passenger service to Boca Grande, which later became another busy port for the Seaboard. On the left is the second CH&N station and general office building. Once the SAL took over, through-train service to and from New York was extended all the way to Boca Grande with the New York Special tourist train, shown here.

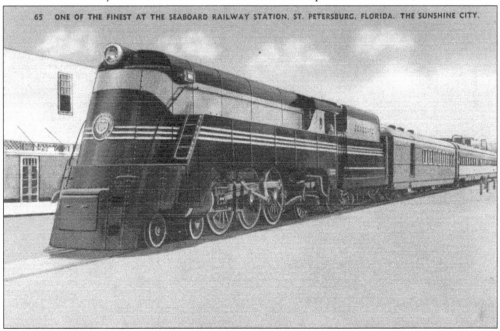

65   ONE OF THE FINEST AT THE SEABOARD RAILWAY STATION, ST. PETERSBURG, FLORIDA, THE SUNSHINE CITY.

Seaboard streamlined several of its 4-6-2 Pacific-type passenger engines in its "citrus" color scheme, which matched that of the new diesels. Although the engine number is not visible, the train, shown at the St. Petersburg station, was likely the west coast section of the Silver Meteor.

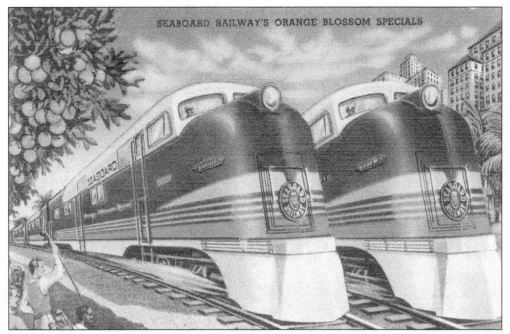

A Silver Meteor promotional postcard showing the two sections (east coast and west coast) of the train attracted innumerable travelers to the new trains. Even though initially made up of coaches, a tavern-lounge-observation car, and a dining car, with no sleeping cars, the trains, which were completely air-conditioned, ran full year round.

Issued to promote service to Camp Blanding prior to World War II, this foldout postcard has a system map, fares, and information relating to the camp and its nearest station, Starke. A number of Florida scenes are part of this promotional piece.

A freight train, powered by one of the newer diesels still in the citrus paint scheme, is passing the rear end tavern-lounge car of the Silver Meteor. With orange groves in the background, the back of the card promotes both the Silver Meteor and "a fleet of fast freight trains."

Postmarked 1908, this postcard shows a passenger train pulling into the Tallahassee station. The station remained essentially unchanged until the end of passenger service on that line. The most famous passenger train on that route was the Jacksonville–New Orleans Gulf Wind.

S A L DEPOT
STARKE, FLA.

The Seaboard updated facilities as necessary. Here, the remodeled Starke station, the depot closest to Camp Blanding, awaits the next train. In 1967, when this real-photo postcard was made, the station was still served by at least four trains daily to and from Jacksonville. Note the REA Express (née Railway Express Agency) truck backed in at the end of the station.

S. A. L. Depot, Ocala, Fla.

Although a union station would later be built for the railroads serving Ocala, this postcard features the SAL's depot in that city. This view must be quite early in the 20th century as the hacks at left are all horse-drawn, with no internal combustion vehicles in sight.

The Seaboard, as part of the Miami extension project, built what was originally called Grand Central Station at 2206 Northwest Seventh Avenue in Miami, which was befitting its status not only as "the magic city" but also as the great up-and-coming Florida metropolis. When it first opened, and for some years after, the station contained division offices, ticket offices, a lunchroom, barbershop, shoe shine parlor, and other stores.

The trackage shown in this postcard skirting Lake Virginia in Orlando was part of the Seaboard branch line that ran from Orlando to Oviedo. The message on the front of the card notes that there are "very beautiful homes on this lake."

39

Sometime in the mid-1950s, management decided that the citrus paint scheme being used on the diesels was too expensive to maintain. The paint scheme used for the passenger diesels thereafter was a simplified one-color arrangement with a red stripe originating at the shield on the front of the engine and continuing to the rear on either side. Published as a postcard by Mary Jayne's Railroad Specialties, this view of E7A No. 3047 was taken at the Miami station by the author on January 7, 1966.

In April 1962, Richard Wallin took this photograph of doodlebug No. 2028, which was used on the Tampa to Venice line as the power for the Silver Meteor connection. When built, this unit and its matching mates contained the power unit, a railway post office, and a baggage compartment. The photograph was published as a postcard by Mary Jayne's.

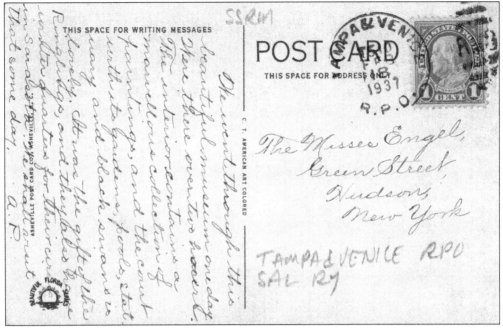

For many years, railroads carried the bulk of all US intercity mail, and almost every railroad in the country had one or more RPOs. Florida was no exception. This postcard was cancelled on the Tampa & Venice RPO train No. 510 on February 18, 1937.

With the merger of the ACL and SAL on July 1, 1967, all-diesel units were repainted to the new railroad's all-black with yellow striping paint scheme. One of the former Seaboard doodlebugs became No. 4900 and was used on the Lakeland to Naples connection for the Champion. It is shown here at Lakeland waiting for its southbound connection, which carried a sleeping car from New York through to Naples.

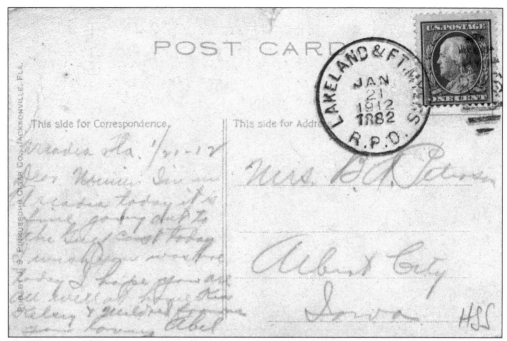

The passenger trains from Lakeland originally went only as far south as Fort Myers, but as the state grew, service was extended to Naples. This postcard was cancelled on the Lakeland & Fort Myers RPO train No. 82 on January 21, 1912, and is now more than 107 years old.

When Amtrak took over the passenger train service of most American railroads, it ended many of the lesser-used and branch line trains, but Florida kept several services, including the Champion, the former ACL/FEC train as a New York–Florida west coast service, complete with the rounded-end tavern-lounge-observation car. Gliding through Lake Alfred, Amtrak No. 86 is en route to St. Petersburg. Richard J. Allen took this postcard photograph, published by Audio-Visual Designs.

Four

Louisville & Nashville Railroad, St. Louis & San Francisco Railway, and Southern Railway

The astute reader might be tempted to ask why the three major railroads in this chapter's title are grouped together, and the answer is simple: although major American railroads, those three, which are referred to in this book as Florida's "secondary big three," were not major carriers in Florida. The mileage of each was a good bit less than any of the primary big three's trackage. While the Southern Railway did originate and terminate several trains in Palatka and Jacksonville, any equipment going farther south was carried mostly by the FEC and, in one case, by the Florida Sunbeam, a short-lived Midwest to Florida train, by the Seaboard.

The St. Louis–San Francisco Railway (the Frisco) operated in Florida from the Alabama border to Pensacola. The first station south of that border was Barrineau Park, and the railroad had approximately 30 miles of track in the Florida Panhandle. However, its famed passenger train, the Kansas City–Florida Special, operated from Kansas City to Birmingham on the Frisco and then continued to Jacksonville on the Southern Railway with through cars to Miami in the winter season via FEC.

The Louisville & Nashville Railroad also entered Florida at the very western end of the Panhandle, its first two stations being Century and Cantonment before reaching Pensacola. From there, the trackage went east, connecting with the Seaboard at Chattahoochee, also known as River Junction. Another short branch left that line at Crestview and connected with the rest of the L&N system at Duvall, Alabama, where yet another line went southeast into Florida and terminated at Graceville. Besides the two daily passenger trains between Jacksonville and New Orleans via the Seaboard and the L&N, the L&N operated numerous name trains that connected with either the ACL or the FEC at Jacksonville, those two railroads bringing the trains south to St. Petersburg, Tampa, or Miami to complete their journeys.

Both the Frisco and the L&N had good-sized facilities at the Port of Pensacola. The L&N's predecessor in Florida, the Gulf, Florida & Alabama (GF&A), built this massive, electrically operated coal pier with a capacity of 600 tons per hour. It was, of course, taken over by the L&N when that road bought the GF&A.

This GF&A postcard showing its docks in Pensacola was cancelled in 1918. Note the variety of buildings and ships; there are at least seven sailing ships visible.

L. & N. R. R. Docks, Pensacola, Fla

While this postcard may appear to be an exact duplicate of the previous view, it is not. The dedicated railroad buff or Pensacola memorabilia collector will note the difference immediately. While the picture is the same, the "G.F.&A. Docks" has been replaced by "L.&N.R.R. Docks" in this 1920-postmarked card. The postcard manufacturers were moving extraordinarily fast!

This unusual postcard view from Pensacola Bay looks north toward the L&N Docks. On the front, the docks are described as "the finest in the world."

Loading Mahogany Logs from Water to Cars, Pensacola, Fla.

Florida had, for many years, a huge logging industry. For a while, the logs from forests north of the west end of the Panhandle were floated into Pensacola Harbor and then placed on flatcars for shipment, as shown here. This is the L&N dock because the building in center background is the same as that shown in two previous postcards.

Mahogany Log Boom and L. & N. Wharfs, Pensacola, Fla.

Here is yet another postcard view with the same building as shown previously, but depicted from the land side, the extent of the L&N's (née GF&A) facilities in Pensacola. The entire former L&N Railroad is now part of CSX Transportation.

"Wish you were here!" This wonderful postcard features a delightful scene with the L&N tracks in the foreground passing Chico Yacht Basin as it crosses Pensacola Bayou.

Once the GF&A established operations in Pensacola, the railroad built this ornate Gingerbread-style station; however, by the time this postcard was produced, it was part of the L&N. The likely reason for the size of this station would have been, as with the CH&N in Boca Grande, that it was also the GF&A's general office.

Eventually, the former GF&A depot became outmoded, and the L&N tore it down and built this new and, for the time (likely the late 1930s), modern station. While the stores on the left side have different names, the station location appears to be unchanged.

Fascinating phraseology is written on this Frisco-published advertising postcard. The second sentence in the copy at upper right states that "Pensacola is the Frisco's port to and from the Seven Seas." As the railroad's map in the Official Guide of the Railways shows, it also reached Mobile, Alabama, but it is possible that it did not have a direct port connection there.

NEW FRISCO DEPOT, PENSACOLA, FLA.

Although the Frisco's passenger train service into Pensacola was minimal, the railroad built a uniquely designed station to serve those using its trains. This white border postcard was mailed in 1931.

18592   THE KANSAS CITY-FLORIDA SPECIAL NEAR ADAMSVILLE, ALABAMA   "ON THE FRISCO"

While most historians and railroad buffs associate the Fred Harvey name with the Santa Fe Railway, the Harvey Company published a wide range of postcards, including this one. Although the location is near Adamsville, Alabama, "on the Frisco," the train shown is the famous Kansas City–Florida Special and is shown here en route to Birmingham and its connection with the Southern Railway, which would take the train to Jacksonville.

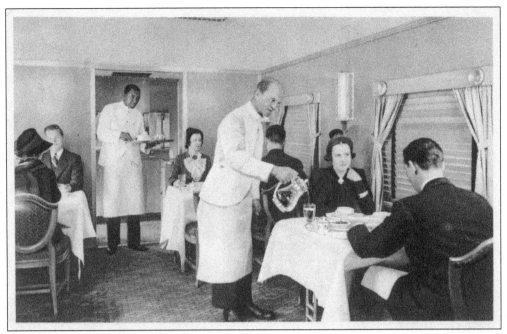

While generally noted for such trains as the Meteor, the Firefly, the Texas Special, and others, the Frisco promoted the Kansas City–Florida Special heavily with sleeping car, lounge, and fine dining car service. This postcard features waiters serving passengers aboard that train. The rear of the card has a full paragraph describing the train's onboard services.

Another Kansas City–Florida Special promotional postcard features the fireplace in the lounge car. The message on the back, advising the traveler to call the Frisco's office in Kansas City to make reservations, notes that "the fireplace adds a homey touch."

Up The Suwanee River~shows G.& F. S. Railway Bridge, Florida

Southern Railway's subsidiary, the Georgia Southern & Florida (GS&F) Railway, operated two lines from Valdosta, Georgia, into Florida, one into Palatka and one into Jacksonville. The Southern had its own line into Jacksonville and served such locations as Asheville, North Carolina, with the Skyland Special. To reach Palatka, the GS&F had to cross the fabled Suwannee River; its bridge over that bucolic waterway is shown here.

A 15142 West Bay Street, Jacksonville, Fla.

Feb. 11 "1906

There are many examples of rare postcards, but among the rarest are those showing any railroad's city ticket offices. The GS&F Jacksonville city ticket office was at 201 West Bay Street, and this postcard, cancelled in Jacksonville in 1906, is extremely rare.

The Southern Railway was mainly famed for its high-grade and high-class passenger train service from New York and Washington to Atlanta, Birmingham, and New Orleans as well as from Cincinnati to Atlanta and New Orleans. However, over the years, the road operated a number of fine Florida trains. One of those, the Florida Sunbeam, which operated in competition with the various entrenched services between the Midwest and Florida, lasted only a few seasons. It was diesel powered between Cincinnati and Valdosta and then, apparently, was hauled by GS&F steam locomotives to Jacksonville, where it was turned over to the Seaboard to complete the trip to Miami.

In the late 1940s, the Southern collaborated with the New York Central and the Florida East Coast on a new Midwest to Florida streamliner named the New Royal Palm. The train was an immediate success, but in 1954, supposedly due to a disagreement on the revenue proportions between the railroads, it was discontinued. "Azalea," the streamlined Pullman tavern-lounge-observation car that the FEC bought for the train, is now the company's office car.

Five

The Short Lines

The short line railroads in Florida not only still exist but also thrive in several cases. For the most part, short line railroads have served a vital function, like serving as a connection to a major railroad over a line or former branch that might not have been profitable for the big road.

As the years went by and the economy changed, a number of short lines in Florida, including Marianna & Blountstown and several others, could not sustain their operations and were shut down by the owners, while others, like the South Georgia and the Live Oak Perry & Gulf (LOP&G), merged and were taken over by Norfolk Southern Corporation and then sold to a short line operator still running as the Georgia & Florida Railroad.

The two major short line operations in the Panhandle are the Bay Line (formerly Atlanta & St. Andrews Bay Railroad) and the Apalachicola Northern (AN) Railroad, both in a rebuilding process following the devastating hurricane of 2018. Several short lines are operating in Central Florida, including Florida Central, Florida Midland, and Florida Northern, all owned by the Pinsly Company, a short line railroad operator that started as a scrapper, taking up railroad lines and selling track, ties, and roadbed to other companies. Based in Clewiston, on the south side of Lake Okeechobee, is South Central Florida Express, owned by United States Sugar Corporation (USSC). That road operates over the former FEC branch between Fort Pierce and Lake Okeechobee through a long-term lease with the FEC and, in addition, operates on the former ACL branch from Clewiston west and north to Moore Haven and other points.

The Florida short line railroads serve a vital function, and for the most part, their future is bright.

ARRIVAL OF FIRST TRAIN IN APALACHICOLA APRIL 30, 1907.

BERT PIERCE, PUBLISHER, APALACHICOLA, FLA.

This very rare postcard issued for the arrival of the first train into Apalachicola shows the crowd thronging the terminal area, joyful at the fact that the town was connected to the world by a railroad. About 112 years later, the AN Railroad is still operating.

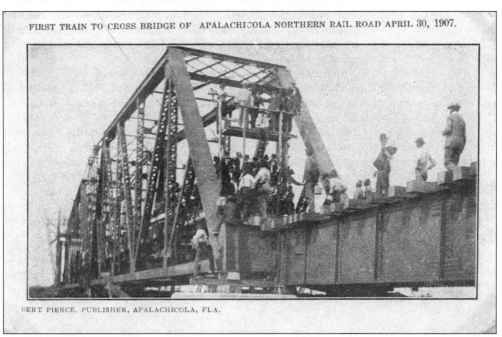

FIRST TRAIN TO CROSS BRIDGE OF APALACHICOLA NORTHERN RAIL ROAD APRIL 30, 1907.

BERT PIERCE. PUBLISHER, APALACHICOLA, FLA.

In conjunction with the arrival of the first train into Apalachicola on April 30, 1907, a special train was operated over the new line. This postcard, as well as the first train into Apalachicola card, was published by Bert Pierce. The author believes that there likely were more images made by Pierce, thus probably more first-day postcards, but has not been able to turn them up.

The title of this sepia-toned postcard is "Scene near Apalachicola Northern R.R. Pier, Port St. Joe, Fla." The pier is visible in the distance.

In July 1948, famed railroad photographer C. William Witbeck made this real-photo postcard of AN 2-8-0 No. 150. The engine, likely in a scrap line, was bought new from the Richmond Works of American Locomotive Company in May 1927.

Mary Jayne Rowe, of Mary Jayne's Railroad Specialties, took this photograph of AN EMD-built road switchers Nos. 714, 716, and 719 on Sunday, September 24, 1978. The three are on the ready track at Port St. Joe, awaiting their next assignment.

In the Florida Panhandle to photograph as many short line operations as possible in order to make postcards, Mary Jayne Rowe took this fine photograph of the Bay Line's EMD-built GP7 road switcher on July 11, 1977. The engine is working the yard, performing switching duties at Panama City.

This black-and-white postcard features the Bay Fisheries Co. building at the end of one of the piers in St. Andrew. The sailing ship *Martha Lillian* is dockside. Crewmen and onlookers are taking in the scene.

In 1906, the Carrabelle, Tallahassee & Georgia Railroad became the Georgia, Florida & Alabama Railroad. In 1927, the line, which ran from points north of Tallahassee south to Carrabelle on the Gulf of Mexico, was leased by the Seaboard. It was abandoned in segments in 1929 and 1948 after serving the people of the area for almost 100 years.

Fellsmere Farms Railroad was built to provide passenger and freight service from beautiful downtown Fellsmere, Florida, to the FEC connection at Sebastian. The railroad would later become the Trans-Florida Central. With declining business, both freight and passenger, the railroad was abandoned in the early 1950s. This very rare real-photo postcard shows the water tank and the maintenance-of-way facilities in Fellsmere.

521 G. Viewing Fellsmere Lands.

This postcard was published by the Fellsmere Farms Company to encourage interested parties to come see the properties available in Fellsmere. The card is postmarked January 12, 1919, and the image shows 4-4-0 No. 100 and a flatcar with what appear to be prospective property buyers seated and standing on the car. The group of musicians at left appear to be a marimba band.

527 B. Fellsmere Farms Company Railroad—Passenger Train.

Fellsmere Farms Railroad No. 100 is coupled to what is likely a Jim Crow passenger car, which is segregated by race, as evidenced by the baggage compartment mid-car. Whether this was an excursion or a regularly scheduled trip is unknown.

FLORIDA RAILWAY BRIDGE ON OLD SUWANNEE, MAYO, FLA.

The Florida Railway was not related to the earlier Florida Railroad, built by David Levy Yulee as the first cross-state railroad. The Florida Railway was a true short line that operated in the north-central portion of the state. A passenger train has apparently stopped on the old Suwanee River bridge near Mayo to allow passengers to take in the scenery or to take photographs if they wished.

JACKSONVILLE GAINSVILLE + GULF #60 5-'40

While it can be considered a predecessor of the Southern Railway's GS&F, the Jacksonville, Gainesville & Gulf (sometimes known as the Gainesville & Gulf) went through a series of machinations through the years, run by a series of owners. Eventually, however, the last 35.9 miles of the railroad were abandoned in 1944. This rare real–photo postcard of 4-6-0 No. 60 was made in May 1940 at Gainesville. The locomotive eventually went to New York State, where it became Unadilla Valley Railroad No. 6.

Though a bit dark, this photograph postcard, possibly taken at twilight, is worthy of inclusion. Showing the diamond-stack 4-6-0 No. 101 of the Live Oak, Perry & Gulf with a full head of steam, the photograph was taken at Perry on August 24, 1933. It should be noted that the locomotive was a wood-burner, and the tender was loaded with that commodity as fuel.

60

With no information on the back of this real-photo postcard, there is no indication of date or location. What is known, however, is that this is Live Oak, Perry & Gulf 2-6-2 No. 103 with steam up and ready to work. Unlike the No. 101 this engine was a coal burner.

Published by the Land Department of the LOP&G, this fine view shows the freight and passenger stations of the railroad with promotional information regarding land and industrial opportunities along the line printed on both the front and back. The card was published in 1913 and is dated April 21 of that year.

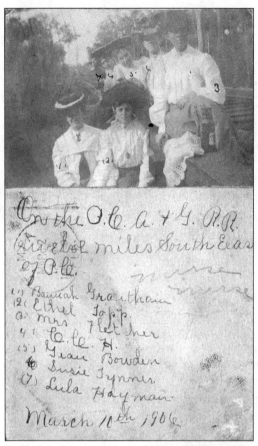

"On the Plant City, Atlantic & Gulf R.R.," this real-photo postcard, taken 12 miles south of Plant City, was mailed from there to Tampa on March 10, 1906. Interestingly, the seven women shown in the photograph are all named below the image. Although difficult to tell for certain, the building behind them appears to be a railroad station. (Plant City is directly east of Tampa.)

The South Georgia Railroad crossed the state line and terminated in Perry, where it connected with the LOP&G. Wood burner 2-6-0 No. 103 is shown working at Perry on August 12, 1933.

SOUTH GEORGIA 103 10-17-52

It is October 17, 1952, and South Georgia No. 103 is still on that railroad's property. It does appear, though, that the engine is out of service and may be waiting for a final determination as to its fate.

SOUTH GEORGIA RY M-100 PERRY FL 12-23-'52

Most of the short line railroads, in Florida and nationally, employed master mechanics who were geniuses not only at keeping the cars and locomotives running but also at buying equipment and adapting it for use on their lines. A perfect example is South Georgia M-100, a passenger, baggage, mail, and express unit obviously rebuilt from another vehicle, possibly a bus. A crewman is ready to climb aboard late in the afternoon of December 23, 1952. The car is in Perry, Florida, in front of the South Georgia Grocery Co., awaiting departure for Perry and possibly points in South Georgia.

Deepest Cut in Florida.
·Tampa Northern Railroad, at Brooksville.

Pub. by Butterweck's Department Store.

The Tampa Northern cut—here being built—was supposedly the deepest in Florida. A short line with grand ambitions for growth, it was taken over by the Seaboard in 1912.

Concluding this chapter is a true short line gem. While the writing on the letterboard on the passenger car is too indistinct to positively identify the railroad, and the locomotive is positioned in such a manner that the name cannot be read, this railroad is added to the list of Florida railroad mysteries. So many questions surround this image. Was it the ACL or SAL? Why was the line abandoned after only a few years when the FEC ended passenger and mixed train service to East Palatka and Palatka and substituted a "bus-truck?" Why are there no known pictures of that vehicle? Questions such as those are what make the study of Florida's railroads all the more fascinating, if not completely intriguing!

Six

INDUSTRIAL, LOGGING, MINING, AND PORT RAILROADS

Florida, particularly in the late 19th and early 20th centuries (and even into the early 1950s), was a haven for the railroad photographer seeking to record the type of railroad operations named in this chapter's title. Almost innumerable, the industrial roads, logging and lumbering railroads, mine rail lines, and railroads owned and operated by several Florida seaports were abundant fodder for the lensman or woman.

It is important, though, for the reader to remember that the content of this book, as all books in Arcadia's Postcard History Series are expected to be, is postcards, and indeed, a large number of the operations named in the title, while well photographed, never had postcards published showing their locomotives, cars, or facilities. If one's favorite company is not shown, please keep in mind that it is entirely possible that no postcards were ever produced showing the day-to-day activity of that company. An excellent example is Peavy–Wilson Lumber of Holopaw.

In 1947, upon the opening of its Fort Pierce cutoff, the FEC ended service on its line from New Smyrna Beach (NSB) to the east side of Lake Okeechobee north of a point known as "Marcy." Although common carrier service was no longer in effect, Peavy–Wilson was given trackage rights at a minimal cost over much of the branch, from NSB to well south of Holopaw, so that the company could continue its logging and lumbering operations. Using its own steam locomotives and equipment, Peavy–Wilson interchanged outgoing freight cars carrying lumber at NSB with the FEC until the region was logged out sometime in 1952 or 1953. While the Peavy–Wilson operation was well photographed, the author has yet to find a postcard showing it. Regretfully, that is the case with many (and perhaps most) of the industrial, logging and lumbering, mine, and port railroads in Florida.

Harvesting Pineapples,
Florida.

Harvesting Pineapples, Florida.

To begin this chapter, here are two postcards that are definitely rail-related but of the on-site agricultural variety. Florida was, and to some degree still is, a major truck (produce) and fruit producer. To many people's surprise, pineapples were a major cash crop for many years, particularly in Dade and what, in 1915, would become Broward Counties. This view of a cart loaded with pineapples was published by the H&WB Drew Company of Jacksonville as part of its Florida Artistic series. What makes it so fascinating, besides the character studies of the men standing on either side of the rail cart, is that the rails appear to be wooden, which was the case in the very earliest years of railroading, prior to iron and later steel rails being used.

This, another view of some kind of narrow-gauge railroad in agricultural use, shows six people, including one woman, loading baskets of pineapples onto the flatcar. The track behind the flatcar is well laid, complete with rails on wooden crossties on a well ballasted roadbed. As with the previous card, the location is unidentified. Neither this nor the previous postcard were mailed.

United States Sugar Corporation (USSC) is based in Clewiston, which refers to itself as "America's Sweetest Town." This linen postcard features four USSC views of the harvesting, collection, transfer from field wagons to railroad cars, and, at bottom right, the movement of the loaded railcars to the USSC sugarhouse for processing. USSC is the only sugar company in North America that owns and operates its own railroad.

The largest raw sugar mill in the United States is operated by USSC in Clewiston. The general layout of trackage is shown on the right side, in the center, and at the left of this postcard.

USSC's sugarhouse is the mill that processes raw sugar. Directly in the center of this postcard is one of the company's EMD-built SW-type switch engines, which is kept busy day and night in the growing season.

This early 1950s postcard shows boxcars on the track to the right of the sugarhouse. The caption on the back of the card states that the sugarhouse is surrounded by 30,000 acres of raw cane fields.

USSC maintains a large fleet of sugarcane railroad cars, which are similar to railroad hopper cars. While a group of visitors on the right is being taken on a tour of the plant, a mounted crane is unloading sugar car No. 578 at the left.

A USSC EMD SW-type diesel switch engine, shown on the right side of the postcard, is moving a trainload of sugarcane cars into the sugarhouse (in the distance) for processing. At left, a string of railroad boxcars is waiting to be loaded with large bags of processed sugar.

Mary Jayne's produced this fine postcard view of USSC GP-7 No. 756 at the company's Clewiston rail shop. The engine was originally built for the ACL as its No. 168, and later became SCL No. 756, which it retained when sold to USSC. The photograph was taken on February 23, 1977.

Florida Power & Light Co. (FP&L) operated two railroad power cars, one of which was based in Miami. In addition, the company owned several diesel locomotives, one of which is shown here. This postcard is a true anomaly because the locomotive bears two different numbers! This locomotive was originally SAL No. 1513 but then became SCL No. 1102, the number shown on the side number boards. However, the number over the headlight is No. 38723, which might be an FP&L property number. The photograph was taken at the company's plant near Indiantown, Florida, in October 1975.

Nelson Blount loved steam locomotives and built Steamtown, USA, in Vermont. The operation moved to Scranton, Pennsylvania, after his passing, and is now part of the National Park Service. It was in Vermont that F.G. Bailey caught Florida-based Brooks–Scanlon Lumber Co. 4-4-2 No. 1 on the turntable. This postcard is undated.

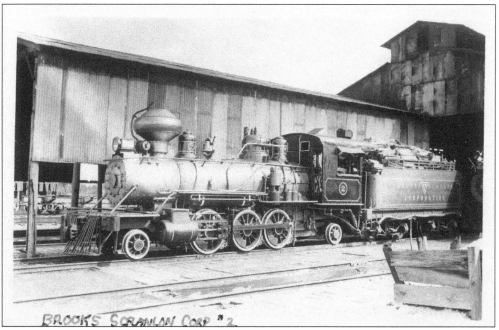

"At home" in Florida, Brooks–Scanlon Corporation 2-6-2 No. 2 was the subject of this real-photo postcard, taken at a company shop (location unidentified) and undated. The locomotive, with a tender filled with wood, is definitely still in service. The original photograph was taken by Bill Witbeck.

The first Train into Lynn Haven, Fla.

It is possible that R.E.L. McAskill & Co. was the contractor that built the line into Lynn Haven, a city in Bay County north of Panama City. Robert E. Lee McAskill, following in his father's footsteps, owned a number of businesses in the Panhandle, including an automobile dealership and several logging and lumber companies. This undated postcard shows the McAskill engine, 4-4-0 No. 2, pushing the first train into Lynn Haven.

Another extremely rare real-photo postcard shows Wilson Cypress Co. 0-6-0 P No. 3 with one man in the cab, two on the gangway, and eight more posing on the slope-back tender for the photographer. Headquartered in Palatka, the company had a number of operations, mostly in northeast Florida.

On display in Bradenton, this 2-8-2 wood-burner served many owners. Its lineage is fascinating. Built in 1913 for the Taylor County Lumber Co., it was sold to Brooks–Scanlon Corp. in Foley and then to Manatee Crate & Lumber Co. in Bradenton. At the end of its career, it was sold to the city of Bradenton, and in August 2002 was moved to the Manatee Historical Village. On display outdoors for many years and not under cover, it began a slow process of deterioration prior to being moved to the village.

The previous view of the several-owner 2-8-2 in Bradenton shows the fireman's side. This postcard shows the engineer's side after the engine was painted and spruced up. The engine is truly a tribute to the great days of steam railroad logging and lumbering in Florida.

Although focused on the Century Mill in the Panhandle's Century, Florida, the trackage and trestlework leading to the mill are clearly visible. The logging railroad that served the mill was the Alger–Sullivan Lumber Company.

Lumbering in a Cypress Swamp, Florida.

Postmarked in Daytona Beach on February 19, 1912, this color postcard shows, as its title notes, "Lumbering in a Cypress Swamp, Florida." There are no markings on either what appears to be a 4-4-0 locomotive or the equipment, but the scene is fascinating nonetheless. A steam crane behind the flatcar is loading logs into a wood-sided railcar for transport, and a careful look reveals that two men are standing on the log that is about to be placed onto or into the railcar.

This marvelous view of a "logging train pulling out for the coast near Pensacola, Fla." was published by the International Post Card Co. in New York. As many postcards of the time were, it was printed in Germany and is undated. The wood-burning engine is a 4-4-0, and it is likely the logs were destined for the L&N lumber dock in Pensacola.

Ellenton, on the Florida west coast, was home to Fuller's Earth Works, shown here. Fuller's earth is a powder used to treat oily skin, and the company is still in business. Its products are sold at many stores and drugstores. The track in the foreground was likely under construction, as indicated by the pile of ties to the right.

Mining Fullers Earth near Quincy, Gadsden County, Fla.

A very small 0-4-0 on what looks like narrow-gauge track is likely backing the several cars shown into position to be loaded with Fuller's earth. Taken in Quincy in Gadsden County near Tallahassee, this real-photo postcard shows the crane mining the mineral. While at least eight men in the background are waiting to put their shovels to work, foreman Moishe Poopick made sure he was front and center for the photograph.

PHOSPHATE MINING NEAR FORT MEADE, FLA.

Although difficult to make out, the 4-4-0 in this 1907-postmarked card is lettered for Palmetto Phosphate. The photograph was taken at the mill in Fort Meade.

For a number of years, from sometime in the 1940s until the mid-1950s, the Miami Municipal Railway operated several "critters," unique and unusual locomotives, to switch the area from near the Seaboard station in Miami to the several Miami docks served by the SAL. One of those engines weighed 40 tons and had rubber tires so that it could cross streets. The engine shown here, possibly a Whitcomb 4-4-0, is being moved by Leonard Bros. Transfer of Miami in order to be put into service.

For the American bicentennial, the Port of Palm Beach, still very much in operation and still operating its own locomotives, repainted one of its EMD-built SW switchers into this patriotic paint scheme. The photograph was taken by the port for distribution to visitors and shippers.

Although all rail switching at Port Miami and Port Everglades is now done by the FEC, Broward County Port Authority operated its own railroad for many years. No. 400 is shown at the port in March 1964 ready to go to work.

For several years, Dr. O.G.J. Schadt operated special passenger cars on express trains between Jacksonville and New York in the winter and spring. An exceptionally rare card, the advertisement on the back notes that the cost of "Special Party Trips" between the two cities was $16, but there were no stopovers or Pullman sleepers with that fare!

Seven

DEPOTS

Like most other states, Florida had a wide variety of depots and stations. In railroad terminology, a depot would indicate a physical building while the word station could refer to either a physical facility or simply a paved or graded or mowed area where a train would stop on signal either to unload passengers or to entrain those waiting who had flagged the train, generally with a white handkerchief during the day or a flashlight or lantern at night.

Florida's physical depots, other than the union stations, which are covered in the next chapter, ranged from very small and utilitarian buildings to unique, unusual, and even elegant structures. Depots and stations in Florida were actually constructed through 1960, and when the FEC strike began in January 1963, that railroad had already drawn up the plans for its new Miami station. Amtrak, taking over most US rail passenger service on May 1, 1971, did build a number of new stations nationwide, including fairly good-sized facilities in Jacksonville and Miami, among others.

Unfortunately, and all too often, the passenger stations, with no trains serving them or with service severely reduced, were torn down; in some cases, particularly Hollywood and Daytona Beach, neither of which was torn down by the railroad, the demolition was an architectural crime. Thankfully, a fair number have been preserved, even if for other than railroad uses. Fortunately, the memories, photographs, and postcards of many of them survive.

As with other chapters, the reader is asked to keep in mind that a selection had to be made that would cover as much of the state as possible. In this chapter, the stations selected, with the exception of the FEC stations, which are shown geographically from north to south, are primarily shown alphabetically.

A. C. L. R. R. Depot, Arcadia, Fla.

Still in use for other purposes, the ACL station in Arcadia was a "solid as a rock" brick building. It served as both a freight and passenger depot.

Avon Park, on the ACL's line to Everglades City and Clewiston, was a regular stop for several passenger and mixed trains. The most famous of those trains was the Scenic Highlander, which for several years carried a sleeping car and a lounge car for the trip to and from Jacksonville.

Seaboard's (and later SCL's) Baldwin station was a regular stop for most passenger trains heading to and from Jacksonville. This is not the original station.

Barrineau Park, noted in the previous chapter, which included the Frisco, was that railroad's first station in Florida on the line from Amory, Alabama, to Pensacola. Although it never handled more than one passenger train (later a mixed train with both freight and passenger service) daily, it was still doing business in 1954.

C. H. & N. R. R. DEPOT. BOCA GRANDE, FLA.

C. F. Kuster, Publisher.

This is the original Charlotte Harbor & Northern depot in Boca Grande. A most unusual layout, it was both a freight and passenger station.

DEPOT AND GENERAL OFFICES, C. H. & N. RY., BOCA GRANDE, FLA.

Still an independent road not yet subsumed by the Seaboard, the CH&N built this sizable station and general office building in Boca Grande. Apparently quite recently opened when the photograph was taken and the postcard made, a considerable number of people are included in this image, published by C.T. (Curt Teich) American Art.

Bradenton's depot was complete with a tower and an open-air and enclosed waiting area. Originally ACL, this building became SCL with the ACL–SAL merger in 1971.

Here is another of the phosphate region stations, this one in Bradley, shown on this 1978 real-photo postcard. An unincorporated community, it was named for Peter B. Bradley, who chartered the Charlotte Harbor & Northern Railway in 1905. Both the original CH&N route and the SAL's line are still in operation, now part of CSX Transportation.

Burnett's Lake station was a well-built brick structure. In Alachua County, the station was fairly close to Gainesville, which is the home of the University of Florida.

L&N DEPOT 1976
COTTONDALE, FLA.

On the L&N's line west of River Junction, Cottondale was a regular stop for most passenger trains operating between Tallahassee (home of both Florida State and Florida A&M Universities) and New Orleans. Looking forlorn and shabby in this 1976 view, the station did not have many years left.

Cross City, the county seat of Dixie County, was served by the ACL. Although sans passenger trains, it was still maintained as a freight station into the 1970s.

A. C. L. DEPOT, CRYSTAL RIVER, FLA,

This extraordinarily rare view of Crystal River features, at center, an ACL 2-6-0 with train in tow loading passengers. This card was cancelled in 1916. On Florida's west coast, in Citrus County, the city considers itself the heart of the nature coast. The Plant System entered the then-unincorporated village in 1888.

Another rarely (if ever) seen postcard is this LOP&G advertising (on back) card featuring a train—and an automobile—at Day on April 14, 1913. The engine is a 4-4-0 wood-burning American Standard type.

The ACL line from Everglades City north to the junction with the mainline was originally built as the Deep Lake Railroad. The Coast Line bought it and began regular freight and passenger service to Everglades City, shown on this chrome postcard after it had been long abandoned and converted to a restaurant. Everglades City is one of the southernmost points on Florida's southwest coast.

The first of two Fort Meade postcards shows the original station building complete with its Southern Express Company sign under the station name. Fort Meade, the oldest city in Polk County, had an animal-powered streetcar at one time. Because Southern Express Company was owned by Henry Plant, it is known that Fort Meade was originally served by the Plant System and then the ACL.

Later, the station in Fort Meade was built using bricks. By the time this photograph was taken, after 1971, the SCL had taken over. Note that the station's semaphore is still in operation—the two arms being straight up meant the incoming train did not have to stop.

Here is another two-era comparison; this one is of Fort Myers. On the Plant System, this card shows a five-car passenger train complete with baggage car and railway post office. The photograph for the card, likely taken after 1902, would indicate that this was an ACL station.

The wooden Fort Myers station on the previous card was replaced in the 1920s when the ACL bought the SAL's line from Fort Myers south to Naples and Collier City, now known as Marco Island. This beautiful Spanish-style building is still in place and is now used for other purposes.

Depot, Largo, Fla.

Largo is in Pinellas County north of St. Petersburg. This wooden building, the ACL's combined freight and passenger station, is now long gone.

S AND DEPOT, LEESB

LEESBURG

At one time, Leesburg had both an ACL and an SAL depot a half mile apart. Since this postcard was postmarked on December 18, 1914, it is likely safe to surmise, since World War I was two years in the future for the United States, that the men in the picture, most in uniform and with rifles, were some sort of reserve or National Guard unit.

A. C. L. Depot, Ocala, Fla.

Before the ACL and the SAL realized and decided that a joint depot at Ocala made more sense than having two separate stations, each road maintained its own depot. The ACL station is shown here.

S.A.L. Depot, Ocala, Fla.

Cancelled in what looks like 1911, the Ocala Seaboard station was, on the day the photograph for this postcard was taken, "a madhouse." There are at least 11 carriages and surreys visible and nary a horseless carriage in sight.

Famed American pioneer aviator Glenn Curtis was instrumental in building several of Miami's western suburbs in the 1920s. Among those was Opa Locka, with its "Arabian nights" theme. For the extension to Miami and the inauguration of the famed Orange Blossom Special, Seaboard president S. Davies Warfield had the Opa Locka station built in concert with Curtis's concept and theme for the city.

The City of St. Petersburg lost its heart and soul when, in the mid- to late 1950s, the famous Webb's City, "the world's largest drug store," went out of business, and both the ACL and the SAL moved their stations out of downtown, with the Coast Line well north and the SAL west and south. Both of those beautiful then-new stations are now gone, but the delightful, modernistic new Seaboard station was memorialized by the company with this dual-view card.

Sorrento is an unincorporated community in Lake County, part of greater Orlando. Neighboring Mount Plymouth is considered part of Sorrento. In this great real-photo postcard, an ACL train is at the depot. Note the barefoot boys at the end of the train, one on the steps and one on the ground—it is "rural Florida in the flesh!"

The FEC segment begins with the road's farthest eastern station, located at Atlantic Beach on the Jacksonville Beaches branch. To the right of the station is the FEC Hotel Company's Continental Hotel, the system's only summer resort. It was a big bust, and the company sold it after only a few years of ownership; several years later, the huge wooden building burned to the ground.

The (pre–Daytona Beach) Daytona station is shown here in 1915. Due to the citizenry's disinterest and neglect, the later station, a beautiful stucco building, was allowed to deteriorate to the point it needed to demolish it, like the station in Hollywood and so many others.

When the Jacksonville, St. Augustine & Indian River Railway reached Rockledge, that town became the end of the line, but only for a short time. The station shown on this postcard, just across the street from the Indian River, was removed shortly after the line was extended farther south.

What became the Orange City branch of the FEC had been the Blue Springs, Orange City & Atlantic Railroad. That company built this beautiful two-story station, with the upstairs likely being living quarters for the station agent and his family. FEC 4-4-0 No. 18 is bringing the three-car train into the station.

Nittaw was on the lonely branch line that ran from New Smyrna Beach through Holopaw and then south to Okeechobee and around the east side of the lake of that name to reach the ACL connection at Lake Harbor. At each location, a depot was built, and most of them were flag stops; some did not even have agents.

FEC DEPOT 1940
WEWAHOTEE, FLA.

WEWAHOTEE

Another great metropolis on the Kissimmee Valley branch was Wewahotee. Of the several stations on the branch, only about eight had agents. Neither Nittaw nor Wewahotee were among them.

Bird's-eye View of Whitehall, Poinciana and Beach Club, Palm Beach, Florida.

The one-mile branch from West Palm Beach to Palm Beach was built to serve the two Flagler System hotels on the island. Because the hotels were open in the winter season only, the Palm Beach station followed the same schedule. Views of that station are quite rare, hence this postcard, showing the station just north of the Royal Poinciana Hotel in the background, was quite a find.

95

The beautiful Hollywood station, built by Joseph Young when he developed the city, was a true architectural gem. Had it survived, it never would have been torn down today.

Ojus was, for many years, an important flag and agency station and was, after Broward became a separate county in 1915, the last station going north and the first coming south in Dade County. It survived until the late 1960s, when it was torn down.

New F. E. C. Depot at Miami, Fla.

Replacing the original Miami station on Sixth Street at the Boulevard, this station opened in December 1912 so that trains would no longer have to back into the station on Sixth Street. After the strike by nonoperating employees began on January 22, 1963, it was torn down between September and December of that year.

Proposed Florida East Coast Railway Depot, Miami, Fla.

Had the FEC strike not begun in January 1963, the railroad was planning to build this ultra-modern passenger terminal on the Buena Vista Yard site, which would have included room for passenger train servicing, with all freight operations being moved to the Hialeah Yard, where they are today.

A. C. L. R. R. Depot, Palm Ave.,
Florida City, Fla.

Florida City was originally known as "Detroit," apparently named by settlers who had moved to that point, the last city or town on the east coast mainland before crossing Jewfish Creek onto Key Largo and the Florida Keys. Somehow the postcard publisher seriously erred, showing the station, with a mixed train awaiting its departure signal (the railroad had not opened to Key West yet), as "A.C.L.R.R. Depot," which it certainly was not!

Eight

UNION STATIONS

The term "union station" refers to a depot or station in a given locale that is served by more than one railroad. The nation's major cities often had such facilities. Buffalo, Detroit, Los Angeles, St. Louis, Dallas, Houston, New Orleans, Portland, Maine, and others offered travelers the convenience of one station in the city rather than requiring them to figure out where their train was arriving or departing from. In addition, the union station enabled those passengers who were changing to trains on other railroads to not have to leave that facility. New York, with Grand Central Terminal and Pennsylvania Station; Chicago, with five stations that had more than one railroad as a tenant and one station with only one railroad operating into and from it; and Atlanta, with two union stations, were the major exceptions as passengers often had to change stations and railroads in those cities to continue their journeys.

Although some Florida cities and towns such as St. Petersburg, Miami, Orlando, and Pensacola did have separate stations, a number of cities had union depots. Jacksonville, of course, was the hub as almost every train operating into and out of Florida either operated through (with a stop, of course) or connected to other trains at that very substantial facility. Tampa Union Station, the second busiest of the union stations in Florida, hosted a number of ACL and SAL trains while other cities, among them Ocala, Kissimmee, River Junction (Chattahoochee), Plant City, and Fernandina did handle trains from more than one railroad at some point in their histories.

Generally, the union stations were a good bit larger than the stations operated by and for only one railroad, but in some cases, the stations outside of the major cities were relatively modest in size. This chapter presents examples of both types.

Union Depot, Jacksonville, Fla.

The main and most important union station in Florida was Jacksonville Terminal. The original building, known as Union Depot and shown here, fronted on West Bay Street. Passengers utilizing it were afforded both through and connecting service. It would eventually become too small and be replaced, although it remained in railroad service, but not handling passenger trains, after 1919, when the new Jacksonville Terminal opened on the same property, just east and south of this building.

Union Depot, Jacksonville, Fla.

A closer view of the Union Depot presents a better perspective of the building, with its arched entranceways. The vehicles shown on the street include both horseless and horse-drawn carriages. Jacksonville Traction Co. streetcar service was available right outside the front door.

The new terminal was an edifice fit for cities far larger than Jacksonville, and newspaper articles of the time described it upon its opening in 1919 as "magnificent." Five railroads—ACL, FEC, GS&F, SAL, and Southern—served it at the time of the station's debut.

With its stately Corinthian columns, the terminal was built to last for the ages. Today, as the Prime Osborne III Convention Center (Osborne was the chairman of SCL and fought for the station's preservation, hence it is fittingly named for him), the building hosts conventions and trade shows, including a major railroadiana and toy train show in February.

Almost until Amtrak moved its Jacksonville station to a new facility north on US 1 at Clifford Lane, the previous station remained in use serving as the mail, baggage, and express loading and unloading facility, with the terminal company's offices on the second floor. The then-new terminal featured almost every service available, from a restaurant and coffee shop to gift shops, a magazine stand, a beauty and barbershop, traveler's aid, and an information booth.

Still quite busy in the 1950s, and with landscaping added, the parking lot in front of the station remained full at most hours of the day and night. As noted previously, almost every train serving Florida passed through or connected at Jacksonville.

This is "Union Depot, Fernandina, Fla." A large crowd is milling about, and the station, north of Jacksonville, served both the town and the Amelia Island resort area. The term "Union Depot" is a bit of a mystery, as only one railroad at a time served the town. The phraseology could be the postcard publisher's (M. Mark, of Jacksonville) literary license.

This late 1910s view of Kissimmee Union Station shows a passenger car being switched and what might be an armstrong (hand-pumped) handcar on the track next to the platform. Passengers are waiting on the platform while the semaphore with an arm perpendicular indicates that an incoming train will be stopping there shortly. The station was served by several Plant System predecessors, hence the union station designation.

UNION STATION, KISSIMMEE, FLA.

Another Kissimmee postcard, published by the Asheville Postcard Co. in the mid-1920, also shows what appears to be a freight train passing through the station. The author believes that the man in the white shirt standing on the platform on the fireman's side of the engine may have been the station agent and was there to hand up train orders to the crew.

L-23. UNION STATION, LAKELAND, FLA.

The second Lakeland Union Station was a large, brick building that eventually would be replaced with a modern edifice that had much more of a Florida look and feel. As with several other union stations in Florida, Lakeland saw service from several ACL predecessors, which were part of the Plant System.

Union Station, Palatka, Fla.

Palatka, which served the GS&F on its west side and the FEC on its east side, also hosted trains of at least two ACL predecessors at one point. As with several of the stations previously shown, Palatka today is a stop for Amtrak trains.

Union R. R. Station, Palatka, Fla.

216292

The FEC, coming into Palatka Union Station on its east side, operated short trains on a regular schedule from East Palatka to Palatka, connecting at the former point with through mainline trains. Eventually, the service was cut back to mixed trains and then to a service operated by a "bus-truck." FEC ended service into Palatka entirely when the St. Johns River bridge was taken out of service in 1947.

Union Depot, Sanford, Fla.

Union Depot in Sanford, north of Orlando, like several other ACL stations, retained that name even after the purchase of the Plant System by the Coast Line. It would not be too long after the 1902 purchase that the predecessor roads would lose their individual identities to become part of ACL.

UNION DEPOT, SEBRING, FLA.

The union depot at Sebring, northwest of Lake Okeechobee, was served by the ACL and the Seaboard. Until the early 1940s, mixed train service was offered from there through Palmdale, two stations south, which was where the branches to Clewiston and Everglades City split from the main line.

Tampa Union Station, designed by Joseph F. Leitner, opened on May 15, 1912, to serve the ACL, SAL, and Tampa Northern Railroads. Hosting daily Amtrak trains today, the station was listed in the National Register of Historic Places in 1974 and was named a local historic landmark by the City of Tampa in 1988.

27—Union Railroad Station
Tampa, Fla.

A Curteich linen, this card was published by Hillsboro News Co. of Tampa. It appears to be either a very late 1940s or early 1950s view of the station; today, it has been fully restored. The City of Tampa, the Community Foundation of Tampa Bay, and the Friends of Tampa Union Station, an all-volunteer group, maintain the station as the local historic jewel that it is.

Nine

FLORIDA'S STREET AND ELECTRIC RAILWAYS

Among railroad buffs, there is a certain faction that will, in the face of evidence to the contrary, stubbornly maintain that streetcar lines are not railroads. While they are certainly entitled to their opinions, the facts belie the validity of that premise. While most of them are electrically operated, so are a number of Class I railroad's mainlines including the former Pennsylvania Railroad between New York and Harrisburg, parts of the former New York Central north of New York City, and the former Illinois Central commuter line in Chicago. Are those operations therefore not railroads? Of course they are!

Streetcar and trolley lines, of which the only one operating in Florida today is in Tampa, with Miami having its Metrorail rapid transit line, are all that is left in the state in terms of electric rail operations, for a number of reasons, most of them due to General Motors and the conspiracy that attempted to destroy America's street and electric railways, which was almost totally successful. However, the history of local streetcar lines in Florida borders on amazing, with passenger conveyances operated electrically, using huge storage batteries or with animal power (horses or mules).

While a number of the Florida streetcar operators did not have the words "railroad" or "railway" in their corporate names, others did, including the Miami Beach Railway Company, St. Petersburg Municipal Railway, and the South Jacksonville Municipal Railway. The Coral Gables Rapid Transit Company even operated a high-speed interurban line between its namesake city and Miami

There are a good many postcards available of the various Florida streetcar and trolley operations, but the purpose of this chapter is to impart the flavor of what local transportation in Florida was like before the streetcar lines were needlessly and ruthlessly destroyed. Clean, quiet, pollution free, and environmentally friendly, it is regrettable that they are not operating today.

The Melbourne Motor Railway operated on Melbourne Beach, providing a unique form of motorized transit on rails for those traveling across the Indian River to enjoy the entertainments on the beach side. Melbourne's Ed Vosatka has written about the line and its history in several publications.

The legendary George Merrick built what was only the second completely planned city in America, Coral Gables. As part of that farsighted endeavor, Merrick incorporated a separate company called the Coral Gables Rapid Transit Co. (CGRT). CGRT operated two main lines between Coral Gables and Miami, one a high-speed interurban line, the other a slower-paced, making-all-stops local streetcar line. One of the big interurbans, No. 2, is shown here on Coral Way, today's Miracle Mile, in front of one of Merrick's striking buildings.

Greater Miami had three separate systems, in Coral Gables, Miami, and on Miami Beach. It was the only place in the state that had all three forms of motive power: animal, battery, and electric. An animal operation was first but was discontinued, and battery cars were installed. After they proved unequal to the job, as they did in all of the Florida cities that tried them, they were replaced with new electric trolleys. A battery-powered car is shown here on Twelfth Street (later Flagler Street) with Florida's most famous department store, Burdine's, on the right.

The Miami Beach Railway Co. operated lines on its namesake city (an island) as well as across the County (later MacArthur) Causeway to and from downtown Miami. A Miami Beach car is entering the Thirteenth Street and Biscayne Boulevard trolley reservation en route to downtown. The building on the left is Sears; the tower was preserved to become part of the Arsht Center, a major arts and entertainment venue in Miami.

Ash Street. Fernandina Fla.

When are you going to work again? Anything in view? I may join you in the summe... Germany

No. 729. Published by Frank W. Simmons Fernandina Fla.

Fernandina, just above Jacksonville, was the farthest north city in Florida to have an electric street railway system. Car No. 510 is on Ash Street and is signed "Beach," meaning that was the destination. This very rare postcard was cancelled in Fernandina on March 13, 1905, making it one of the earliest Florida streetcar or trolley postcards known.

West Bay Street, Jacksonville, Fla.

Jacksonville was served, initially, by both the South Jacksonville Municipal Railway and the Jacksonville Traction Company, the latter being a fairly extensive system. West Bay Street was not only a major thoroughfare, it also had a double-tracked path to Jacksonville Terminal. Car No. 91, on the right, was an "open" car, meaning that passengers could board using the running board visible on the left side of the car and the conductor would collect the fare. The car is signed "Fairfield," which is visible at front center of the car and to the right of the advertising placard.

Palatka, after giving up its animal-powered system, never built an electrified system to replace it. Fortunately, this card, cancelled in Palatka on March 2, 1905, just a few days earlier than the Fernandina card, proves the existence of the operation. The trolley and its motive power are in front of the famed Putnam House Hotel. (Palatka is in Putnam County.)

King Street showing Ponce de Leon, St. Augustine, Fla.

The oldest city in America, St. Augustine, founded in 1565—well before Jamestown—had two electric lines and two horse- or mule-powered streetcar lines, which were on North Beach and Anastasia Island. The St. Augustine & South Beach Railway started as a steam-powered line and was later electrified, while the St. Johns Electric Co. operated several different types of cars in the city. Three of the cars, a closed and two convertibles, are shown in front of the FEC Hotel Company's famed Ponce de Leon Hotel (now Flagler College) in 1910.

Capo's North Beach Rapid Transit was one of St. Augustine's two animal-powered trolley lines. What was so unique about this operation was that the horse walked alongside the open-air trolley, pulling it in a different manner than the normal front-harnessed animal.

Central Avenue, looking North, St. Petersburg, Fla.

On Florida's west coast, St. Petersburg, Tampa, and Bradenton all had electric streetcar systems. St. Pete Municipal Railway and Tampa Electric Co. were each the result of the purchase and amalgamation of predecessors, while Florida Power & Light built and operated the quite small Bradenton line. Central Avenue is St. Petersburg's main east–west dividing street and had streetcars operating on it until 1949, when it became a victim of GM and the conspiracy hatchet job. An open car, boarding and unloading, is shown on the then single track line. To pass, cars used sidings to reach their destinations without incident.

The name of one of the St. Petersburg lines was "Jungle," likely due to the overgrowth of vegetation in that area of the city. Car No. 40 is on that line in this postcard, published by the E.C. Kropp Co. of Milwaukee.

Main Street, Sanford, Fla.

At least four cities in Florida, including Miami, Daytona Beach, Everglades City, and Sanford, had battery-powered streetcar lines, none of which proved to be anything but minimally successful. Sanford's streetcar service was known as "the Celery Belt Line," and its car No. 2 is seen performing its duties on Main Street. Although this card is very early (cancelled February 5, 1912), there appear to be as many automobiles on the street as there are horse-drawn carriages, buckboards, or wagons.

At this time, Tampa is the only city in the state with an operating streetcar line and is planning to expand it. A very interesting postcard, this scene includes a horse-drawn carriage, a number of automobiles in the background, and three open trolleys. In the background is the Tampa Bay Hotel, built by Henry Plant. Today, it houses not only the University of Tampa but also the Henry B. Plant Museum.

Many American cities had "trolley parks," which were built and served by the local streetcar or interurban railway. Florida might have had only one, Tampa's Ballast Point Park. That park was a favorite of Tampans; pictured is its pavilion for boarding and detraining guests.

CAYO HUESO   CARITOS DE MULAS

THE SOUTHERNMOST RAILWAY IN THE U.S.A.
DUVAL STREET   DIVISION STREET   WHITE STREET   POST OFFICE
PORTER DOCKS   MALLORY PIER   THOMPSON FISH WHARF
OPEN CARS
ALL YEAR ROUND   KEY WEST, FLA.   FARE FIVE CENTS
(CINCO CENTAVOS)

What a kick! Sometime in the 1940s, the Electric Railroader's Association, based in New York City, published, through the sponsorship of longtime electric railway advocate E.J. Quinby, at least two whimsical caricature-type postcards commemorating the Key West mule- and later electrically-powered systems. The former was converted to the latter in 1899, and the electric system was abandoned in 1926. This truly one-of-kind postcard is bilingual.

Ten

Tourist Roads, Museums, and Attractions

Over the years, there have been many tourist railroads, railroad museums, and tourist attractions that featured either steam or diesel railroads, generally narrow gauge, as part of their entertainment. For better or for worse, many have closed for various reasons, from changes in the public's interest to economic conditions, but a number of them soldier on.

There have been operations that fall into this chapter's categories from the Panhandle to the first coast (Jacksonville and St. Augustine south to Ormond Beach and Daytona Beach) to Central Florida, the west coast, and the east coast, and in this chapter, readers will have the pleasure of seeing examples of all three types. However, as with the other chapters, not every facility or museum could be included, mostly because of the immensity of the resources available for use and the space allotted in this book.

Among those still in operation are the South Florida Railroad Museum, the Gold Coast Railroad Museum, and of course, Walt Disney World. Interestingly, Disney operates a steam railroad, a horse-drawn trolley, and a monorail simultaneously, all of which have been a part of the park almost since its opening. Finally, mention should be made of United States Sugar Corporation. That company, after operating former FEC 4-6-2s Nos. 113, 148, and 153, and now a fleet of diesel locomotives, is currently in the process—much to the joy of Florida's and America's railroad buffs—of rebuilding FEC No. 148, a 4-6-2, and No. 253, a 0-8-0, for service. In addition, the massive 250-ton steam wreck train crane based at Buena Vista Yard is also in the process of restoration. Happily, it appears that tourist roads, rail-oriented museums, and tourist attractions with some form of railroad-oriented display will be a highlight of the Florida railroad scene for many years to come.

Although now gone, the narrow-gauge steam railroad at Fort Lauderdale's Birch State Park was a major draw. The memory of that one-mile scenic railroad through the park still brings warm smiles to all who remember it.

Crandon Park on Key Biscayne, run by Dade County, was one of the area's top attractions, both for tourists and residents, due in no small part to the Biscayne Bay, Atlantic & Gulf Railroad. That miniature railroad also had about a one-mile run and would stop at the entrance to the Crandon Park zoo to drop off and pick up passengers. Besides the internal-combustion-powered steam engines, the wonderful signs such as "Twain Twack" were equally memorable. Owned by Lester L. Sargent, the district passenger agent of the L&N Railroad in Miami, it operated until—following Sargent's passing, several damaging hurricanes, and the removal of the zoo farther inland—it was simply no longer feasible to continue the operation.

The Gold Coast Railroad originated as the Miami Railroad Historical Society and operated on what was the University of Miami's South Campus on Southwest 152nd Street until it moved to a new location on the north side of the Fort Lauderdale Airport. Blessed with the two ex-FEC and ex-USSC 4-6-2s, the Gold Coast was a major draw. When Interstate 595 was built, the museum was forced to move back to its original Richmond Naval Air Station (the former University of Miami's South Campus) location, and there, it went back into operation. Unhappily, for various reasons, the steam locomotives are now inoperable, and the museum is facing a plethora of operational and fiscal problems.

The Lake Wales, Great Masterpiece & Southern Railway was a 15-inch-gauge line, which operated live-steam locomotives through the jungle at the Great Masterpiece tourist attraction in Lake Wales. As with the Birch State Park Railroad and the Biscayne Bay, Atlantic & Gulf, the LWGM&S did not survive. The steam locomotive shown was modeled after the New York Central Railroad's 4-6-4 Hudson types.

Petticoat Junction Railroad, named for the television show of that name, operated within the like-named attraction near Panama City in the Panhandle. Narrow-gauge 2-6-0 No. 7 was originally built for Argent Lumber Company in South Carolina in 1914 by the H.K. Porter Company. Both the attraction and its railroad are both long gone and are now a part of history.

In Homestead, the Florida Pioneer Museum was opened in what had been the FEC section foreman's house at that point. Eventually, the museum received the last FEC wooden cupola caboose as a donation from the railroad, but due to lack of maintenance, the caboose was moved several years ago to the Gold Coast Railroad Museum, where it is awaiting restoration.

St. John's and Eastern R.R., Mandarin, Fla.

Mandarin, which was the site of the St. Johns & Eastern Railroad, is 13 miles south of Jacksonville on Florida State Road 13. Privately owned by Mr. and Mrs. E.C. Ward, the miniature railroad was open on Sundays and holidays. The Wards, who, like their railroad, are long gone, advertised it as "the greatest train ride in the world for a dime!" The engine shown, on what looks like 15-inch-gauge track, was a live steamer, not internal combustion powered.

Another of the attractions that featured a ride behind a steam locomotive was the railroad at Six Gun Territory in Silver Springs near Ocala. Although a bit difficult to tell with certainty, the track is definitely narrow gauge, likely two feet, six inches. As with the other attractions previously named, Six Gun Territory has been "shot down" and is now, sadly, buried in "Boot Hill."

The Trilby, San Antonio & Cypress (TSA&C) Railroad, also known as the Orange Belt Line because it ran on the roadbed of the former Orange Belt Railway, began operations on July 4, 1976. The line was not ready to handle the steam locomotive it had purchased for service, so when it opened, this General Electric 65-ton center cab diesel, shown with a train between San Antonio and Blanton, was pressed into service.

The TSA&C lasted a little more than a year at Trilby and then moved to Webster, Florida, where it ran a few more months. When the original line was ready, 2-6-0 No. 203 was brought online and immediately went into service.

TSA&C No. 203 was built in 1925 by Baldwin Locomotive Works for the Washington & Lincolnton Railroad in Georgia and was eventually sold to another short line, the Rockton & Rion in South Carolina, which then sold it to the Orange Belt Line. The engine is ready to roll, pulling Pullman sleeping cars "Jovita" and "Overdale." Sadly, this standard-gauge line is also no more.

Trains of Yesterday was envisioned as the great home and gathering spot for both steam locomotives and rare passenger and freight cars. Located in Hilliard north of Jacksonville, and even though operating under the aegis of the American Railroad Equipment Association, it was never a success. After several years, it was closed, and the equipment was sold or scrapped. Here, 0-4-0 No. 2, a tank engine with no tender, is shown with an 1883 passenger car and a former Georgia & Florida Railroad caboose.

As mentioned in this chapter's introduction, Walt Disney World, almost from its opening near Orlando as part of the Reedy Creek Improvement District, operated a horse-drawn trolley route, a steam-powered passenger train, and a monorail. The horse-drawn streetcar, shown here, is operating on Main Street, USA, passing the movie house, then featuring Mickey Mouse in *Steamboat Willie*.

Waiting for passengers in front of the entrance to the Magic Kingdom, a narrow-gauge 4-6-0 was photographed with "steam up" awaiting the highball. The trains carry guests on a one-and-a-half-mile grand circle excursion tour.

Visit us at
arcadiapublishing.com